D1389544

To Jess

From Sue

X

Other books in the TO-GIVE-AND-TO-KEEP™ series:
Wishing you HAPPINESS
To a very special MOTHER
To someone special in TIMES OF TROUBLE
To my very special HUSBAND
To a very special DAD
To a very special SON
To a very special DAUGHTER
To my very special LOVE

Published in 1991 by Helen Exley Giftbooks in Great Britain.
This edition published in 2008

12 11 10 9 8 7 6 5 4 3

ISBN 13: 978-1-84634-204-2

Illustrations by Juliette Clarke. Edited by Helen Exley.
Important Copyright Notice: PAM BROWN, MARION C. GARRETTY, RICHARD
ALAN, H.M.E., JUDITH C. GRANT, MAYA V. PATEL © HELEN EXLEY 1992, 2008
Printed in China.
'TO A VERY SPECIAL'® IS A REGISTERED TRADE MARK OF HELEN EXLEY GIFTBOOKS

Helen Exley Giftbooks, 16 Chalk Hill, Watford, Herts WD19 4BG, UK.
www.helenexleygiftbooks.com

To a very special®
FRIEND

Illustrations by Juliette Clarke.
Edited by Helen Exley.

BY MY SIDE
Don't walk in front of me,
I may not follow.
Don't walk behind me,
I may not lead.
Walk beside me,
And just be my friend.

AUTHOR UNKNOWN

HELEN EXLEY®

WHAT IS A FRIEND?

A friend is a person with whom you dare
to be yourself.

PAM BROWN, b. 1928

A friend is someone who dislikes the same
people you dislike.

ANONYMOUS

...A friend doesn't go on a diet because you
are fat. A friend never defends a husband
who gets his wife an electric skillet for
her birthday. A friend will tell you she saw your
old boyfriend – and he's a priest.

ERMA BOMBECK (1927-1996)

Friend derives from a word meaning "free".
A friend is someone who allows us the space
and freedom to be.

DEBBIE ALICEN

Real friends are those who, when you've
made a fool of yourself, don't feel
that you've done a permanent job.

H.M.E.

THE COMFORT OF SMALL THINGS

Oh, the comfort – the inexpressible comfort,
of feeling safe with a person – having neither
to weigh thoughts nor measure words,
but pouring them all right out, just as they
are chaff and grain together; certain
that a faithful hand will take and sift them,
keep what is worth keeping, and then, with
the breath of kindness blow the rest away.

DINAH MARIA MULOCK CRAIK (1826-1887)

And all people live, not by reason of any care
they have for themselves, but by the love
for them that is in other people.

LEO TOLSTOY (1828-1910)

The happiness of life is made up of minute
fractions – the little soon-forgotten charities
of a kiss or a smile, a kind look,
or heartfelt compliment.

SAMUEL TAYLOR COLERIDGE (1772-1834)

Friends run across the road with a plate
of freshly baked scones.
Friends fetch you to see the newly born kittens.
Friends clear the snow off your side
of the driveway.
Friends stop the papers when you forget.
Friends feed the cat.
Friends are absolutely indispensable.

JUDITH C. GRANT, b. 1960

A friend, by a phone call,
a popping-in,
a chance meeting,
a small unexpected
surprise, puts a little
jam on the day's bread
and butter.

J.R.C.

A FRIEND IS...
A friend knows how to allow for
mere quantity in your talk,
and only replies to the quality....
WILLIAM DEAN HOWELLS (1837-1920)

Friends stay friends because they don't
mess about in each other's lives.
RICHARD ALAN

A friend respects your diet.
PAM BROWN, b. 1928

A friend never says "I told you so"
– even when she did.
WENDY JEAN SMITH

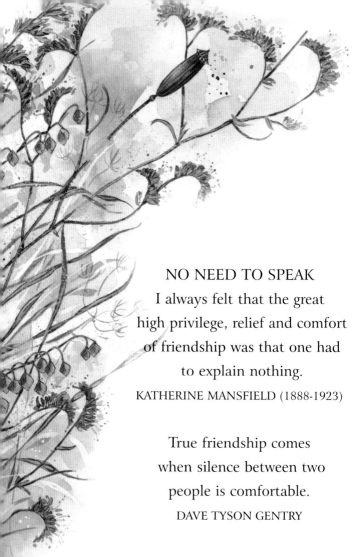

NO NEED TO SPEAK
I always felt that the great
high privilege, relief and comfort
of friendship was that one had
to explain nothing.
KATHERINE MANSFIELD (1888-1923)

True friendship comes
when silence between two
people is comfortable.
DAVE TYSON GENTRY

Silences make the real conversations between friends. Not the saying but the never needing to say is what counts.

MARGARET LEE RUNBECK

A friend hears the song in my heart and sings it to me when my memory fails.

from "Pioneer Girls Leaders' Handbook"

...when people have light in themselves,
it will shine out from them.
Then we get to know each other
as we walk together in the darkness,
without needing to pass our hands
over each other's faces,
or to intrude into each other's hearts.

ALBERT SCHWEITZER (1875-1965)

THAT VERY SPECIAL FRIEND

We cannot tell the precise moment when
friendship is formed. As in filling a vessel
drop by drop, there is at last a drop
which makes it run over; so in a series
of kindnesses there is at last one which makes
the heart run over.

JAMES BOSWELL (1740-1795)

First of all things, for friendship, there must be
that delightful, indefinable state called feeling
at ease with your companion,
the one man, the one woman
out of a multitude who interests
you, who meets your thoughts and tastes.

JULIA DUHRING

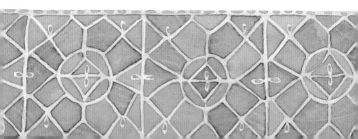

Then little by little we discover one friend,
in the midst of the crowd of friends, who
is particularly happy to be with us and to whom,
we realize, we have an infinite number of
things to say. She is not the top of the class,
she is not particularly well thought of by the
others, she does not wear showy clothes...
and when we are walking home with her
we realize that her shoes are identical to ours –
strong and simple, not showy and flimsy like
those of our other friends....

NATALIA GINZBURG (1916-1991), from "The Little Virtues"

Friends do not live in harmony merely,
as some say, but in melody.

HENRY DAVID THOREAU (1817-1862)

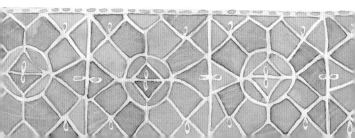

...BY BEING YOURSELF

I love you not only for what you are,
but for what I am when I am with you.

I love you not only for what you have made
of yourself, but for what you are making of me.

I love you because you have done more than
any creed could have done to make me good,
and more than any fate could have done to
make me happy.

You have done it without a touch,
without a word, without a sign.

You have done it by being yourself.
Perhaps that is what being a friend means,
after all.

ROY CROFT

Life is nothing without friendship.

CICERO (106-43 B.C.)

Of all the things which wisdom provides
to make life entirely happy,
much the greatest is
the possession of friendship.

EPICURUS (341-270 B.C.)

Friendship is unnecessary, like philosophy,
like art... It has no survival value;
rather it is one of those things that give value
to survival.

C. S. LEWIS (1898-1963)

Friendship improves happiness,
and abates misery, by doubling our joy,
and dividing our
grief.

JOSEPH ADDISON (1672-1719)

Love is caviar and wedding cake,
strawberries and cream.
Love is champagne.
Friendship is new bread,
fresh butter,
farmhouse cheese and
a pot of tea for two.
Of course, to get through
life, it's best to combine
the two. But friendship
is easier on the digestion.

PAM BROWN, b. 1928

The truth is friendship
is to me every bit as
sacred as eternal marriage.

KATHERINE MANSFIELD (1888-1923)

THANK YOU!
If I were to make a solemn
speech in praise of you,
in gratitude, in deep affection,
you would turn an alarming
shade of crimson and try
to escape. So I won't.
Take it all as said.

MARION C. GARRETTY (1917-2005)

I want just one thing.
To live long enough
to pay back in some way
your undeserved and
overwhelming generosity.

PAM BROWN, b. 1928

The hardest thing
is not to be able to work
magic for a friend.
MAYA V. PATEL, b. 1943

I no doubt deserved
my enemies, but
I don't believe I deserved
my friends.
WALT WHITMAN (1819-1892)

As long as there is a post and the telephone
is not cut off, so long as we have things
to tell and joys and anxieties to share –
we will be friends. Always.

MARION C. GARRETTY (1917-2005)

I think there is, in friendship, an instant
recognition – a kind of loving.
It needs only a word in passing,
the touch of a hand – yet parting is loss, and
the tiny ache of regret stays with us always.

H.M.E.

FAR AWAY

In loneliness, in sickness, in confusion –
the mere knowledge of friendship makes
it possible to endure, even if the friend
is powerless to help.
It is enough that they exist.
Friendship is not diminished by distance
or time, by imprisonment or war,
by suffering or silence.
It is in these things that it roots
most deeply. It is from
these things that it flowers.

PAM BROWN, b. 1928

Here at the frontier, there are falling leaves.
Although my neighbours are all barbarians,
And you, you are a thousand miles away,
There are always two cups on my table.

AUTHOR UNKNOWN,
T'ANG DYNASTY (618-906 A.D.)

QUOTATIONS ABOUT FRIENDSHIP

There's nothing worth the wear of winning,
but laughter and the love of friends.
HILAIRE BELLOC (1870-1953)

"Stay" is a charming word
in a friend's vocabulary.
LOUISA MAY ALCOTT (1832-1888)

The worst solitude is to be destitute
of sincere friendship.
FRANCIS BACON (1561-1626)

But every road is rough to me
that has no friend to cheer it.
ELIZABETH SHANE, fl. 1920s

A TROUBLE SHARED
It is not so much our friends' help
that helps us as the confident knowledge
that they will help us.

EPICURUS (341-270 B.C.)

I never crossed your threshold
with a grief,
but that I went without it.

THEODOSIA GARRISON
(1874-1944)

It is the friends you can call up at 4 a.m.
that matter.

MARLENE DIETRICH (1904-1992)

A friend is someone who arrives when you
have 'flu with a bag of oranges, the thriller
you wanted to read and a bunch of flowers.
They put the flowers in a vase,
make you a hot drink, do the washing up –
and go.

PAM BROWN, b. 1928

When a friend asks there is no tomorrow.

GEORGE HERBERT (1593-1633)

A real friend is one who walks in when
the rest of the world walks out.

WALTER WINCHELL (1879-1972)

SHARING

Grief can take care of itself,
but to get the full value of a joy you must
have somebody to divide it with.

MARK TWAIN (1835-1910)

Happiness seems made to be shared.

JEAN RACINE (1639-1699)

Friends, companions, lovers, are those
who treat us in terms of our unlimited
worth to ourselves. They are closest to us
who best understand what life means to us,
who feel for us as we feel for ourselves,
who are bound to us in triumph
and disaster, who break the spell
of our loneliness.

HENRY ALONZO MYERS

...It is that my friends have made the story of my life. In a thousand ways they have turned my limitations into beautiful privileges, and enabled me to walk serene and happy in the shadow cast by my deprivation.

HELEN KELLER (1880-1968)

What do we live for, if it is not to make life less difficult for each other?

GEORGE ELIOT (MARY ANN EVANS) (1819-1880)